Abide

Abide

Understanding the secrets of living for Jesus

Warren W. Wiersbe

First published in Great Britain in 2016, reprinted 2018

Reprinted by Nørhaven, Denmark 2019

Previously published in 1977 by Tyndale House under the title
5 Secrets of Living

British Library Cataloguing in Publication Data
A record for this book is available from the British Library

ISBN: 978-1-910587-73-7

Designed and typeset by Pete Barnsley (Creative Hoot)

10Publishing, a division of 10ofthose.com
Unit C, Tomlinson Road, Leyland, PR25 2DY, England

Email: info@10ofthose.com
Website: www.10ofthose.com

Dedicated with loving appreciation
to Mr. and Mrs. Clifford Warren, who
gave me my wife

Contents

Preface

LIFE is your most precious possession. Don't take it for granted.

Right now, you are either *wasting* your life, *spending* your life, or *investing* your life. It is *you* who determines which course to follow.

Jesus said, 'The thief comes only to steal and kill and destroy; I have come that they may have life, and have it to the full' (Jn. 10:10).

'The thief ...' Who is he? Ultimately, of course, he is Satan, the enemy of God and of good. But the thief always has assistance from people and circumstances. One man is robbed of life because of impatience: he always jumps the gun, only to find that the gun is aimed at him. Another person is robbed of abundant life because of selfish indulgence – food, sleep, sex, alcohol. You name it. Yes, there are many thieves that would like to keep us from enjoying Christ's abundant life: memories of past failures, fears of the future, a feeling that you're not important and that nobody cares. How tragic going through life and really not living!

But abundant life can be yours.

In his message about the Vine and the branches, Jesus Christ points out five spiritual secrets that lead to abundant life.

Please take these five spiritual secrets to heart: They work!

Warren W. Wiersbe
Moody Church, Chicago, 1977

In the Upper Room, Jesus Spoke These Words to His Disciples:

> I am the true vine, and my Father is the gardener. He cuts off every branch in me that bears no fruit, while every branch that does bear fruit he prunes so that it will be even more fruitful. You are already clean because of the word I have spoken to you. Remain in me, as I also remain in you. No branch can bear fruit by itself; it must remain in the vine. Neither can you bear fruit unless you remain in me.
>
> I am the vine; you are the branches. If you remain in me and I in you, you will bear much fruit; apart from me you can do nothing. If you do not remain in me, you are like a branch that is thrown away and withers; such branches are picked up, thrown into the fire and burned. If you remain in me and my words remain in you, ask whatever you wish, and it will be done for you. This is to my Father's glory, that you bear much fruit, showing yourselves to be my disciples.

*As the Father has loved me, so have I loved
you. Now remain in my love. If you keep my
commands, you will remain in my love, just as I
have kept my Father's commands and remain in
his love. I have told you this so that my joy may
be in you and that your joy may be complete.
My command is this: Love each other as I have
loved you. Greater love has no one than this: to
lay down one's life for one's friends. You are my
friends if you do what I command. I no longer call
you servants, because a servant does not know
his master's business. Instead, I have called you
friends, for everything that I learned from my
Father I have made known to you. You did not
choose me, but I chose you and appointed you
so that you might go and bear fruit –fruit that will
last – and so that whatever you ask in my name
the Father will give you. This is my command:
Love each other.* **99**

(Jn. 15:1–17)

Secret One:

The Secret of Living is Fruitbearing

He cuts off every branch in me that bears no fruit, while every branch that does bear fruit he prunes so that it will be even more fruitful.

This is to my Father's glory, that you bear much fruit ...

You did not choose me, but I chose you and appointed you so that you might go and bear fruit – fruit that will last ...

(Jn. 15:2, 8, 16)

What and who am I? Why am I here?

You must answer these questions correctly if life is to have meaning for you. The man who calls a spanner a screwdriver, and who tries to use it as a screwdriver, is heading for frustration and failure. The person who does not know *who* and *what* he is will experience the same kind of frustration and failure. It is this identity crisis that has threatened and even destroyed many people in society today.

The Christian need not have an identity crisis. Jesus tells us who we are and why we are here. We are branches, and he is the Vine. We are here to bear fruit. Once you accept this simple fact, you are on the way to making your life meaningful and useful.

How did you become a branch in Christ, the Vine? By trusting him as your Saviour and Lord. You have, by faith, a living relationship with Christ. You are not simply a member of a religious group; you are a living branch in the living Vine. When you yielded to Christ, a living union was formed between you and the Lord. Just as the branch gets its life from the vine, so the believer gets his life from Jesus Christ.

If you do not have this living union with Christ, you cannot bear fruit. Fruit is the result of life. You can manufacture religious substitutes, but they will not be fruit.

One of the reasons God saved you is that you might bear fruit in this world. You are living in a hungry world where people are starving for spiritual reality. *The branch does not bear fruit for the branch to eat, but for others to eat.* It is one of the great joys of life to share this fruit with others. That is why we are here.

Fruitbearing is a beautiful process. First there are the leaves; then the flowers; then the fruit. God provides the water from beneath and the sun from above. Day by day the branches develop; day by day the fruit is produced. If you are looking for instant fruitfulness, you will be disappointed. Fruit must be cultivated. As we shall see later, the branch must abide in the Vine and draw upon His abundant life.

So, the reason God made you and saved you is that you might bear fruit in this world. You are a branch and he is the Vine. He has put you where you are that you might accomplish His special purpose. There is fruit to be produced where you are that nobody else can produce but you. *Accept the glory and the responsibility of being one of His branches.*

What is this fruit that God wants us to bear? It takes many different forms.

Winning others to Christ and helping them grow is fruit. Paul wrote to his friends at Rome, 'I planned many times to come to you ... in order that I might have a harvest among you, just as I have had among the other Gentiles' (Rom. 1:13). There are many pictures in the Bible of the ministry of witnessing and leading others to Christ. '[H]e who wins souls *is* wise', states Proverbs 11:30 (NKJV), and that word 'wins' calls to mind a hunter taking his prey. Sometimes we must track down a lost soul in order to 'take him' for Christ. Jesus compared evangelism to catching fish. 'Come, follow me ... and I will send you out to fish for people' (Mk. 1:17). Paul compared the evangelist to an ambassador (2 Cor. 5:20), and Jesus said the soul-winner was a harvester (Jn. 4.35). Zechariah 3:2 pictures the soul-winner as a fireman, snatching a burning brand out of the fire.

All of these pictures are true, because the ministry of leading others to Christ has many facets to it. It is wrong to focus on only one facet, because this will lead to a static, mechanical kind of a witness. There are times when soul-winning is a dangerous, dramatic experience as we snatch the brands out of the fire. At other times, we calmly and patiently sow the seed and ask God for a harvest. Sometimes others work with us and we cast the net into the sea and catch many fish. Again, sometimes we have that personal witness to one soul and as faithful ambassadors share the good news of the gospel.

But in all of these pictures, one factor is constant: *life*. The hunter, the fisherman, the harvester, the fireman, and the ambassador must have *life* if they are to get their work accomplished. This life can only come from Jesus Christ. As we are united to him and abide in him, his life flows in and through us, and we bear fruit. 'I am the Vine, you are the branches.' It is not *we* who do the work; it is he who does it in us and through us. We make ourselves available to him, and he makes his life available to us. Paul expressed it perfectly in 1 Corinthians 15:10: 'I worked harder than all of them – yet not I, but the grace of God that was with me.'

It is a great joy and privilege to lead others to Christ. This ministry is not the automatic result of memorizing verses or passing courses. It is the result of allowing Christ's love to flow through you and bear fruit. 'No branch can bear fruit by itself; it must remain in the vine. Neither can you bear fruit unless you remain in me' (Jn. 15:4).

Another kind of spiritual fruit is *practical holiness of life.* 'But now that you have been set free from sin and have become slaves of God, the benefit you reap leads to holiness, and the result is eternal life' (Rom. 6:22). The theme of Romans 6 is victory over sin, and the fruit of this victory is a holy life. Never think of 'holiness' as a brittle kind of piety such as the Pharisees practiced. Holiness is nothing else but the beauty and character of God displayed in our everyday lives. Holy living means more than victory over sin; it also means growth in character so that we become more like Jesus Christ. It has both negative and positive aspects: 'let us purify ourselves from everything that contaminates body and spirit, perfecting holiness out of reverence for God' (2 Cor. 7:1). As we share the life of Christ, we share the character of Christ.

Many people try to achieve holiness of life by means of some formula or religious discipline. Their system works for a time, and then they experience failure and frustration. Holiness is to the inner man what health is to the outer man; and both of them are a by-product of life. The person who eats properly, exercises, keeps clean and gets the right amount of rest, will usually enjoy good health. The Christian who abides in Christ and shares his life will produce the fruit of holiness. *You cannot manufacture holiness*. The Pharisees tried to do this and Jesus called them hypocrites. Holiness of life must come from within. It is fruit that we bear because we are branches in the Vine.

A third kind of fruit he enables us to bear is *the sharing of what we possess*. When Paul gathered a missionary offering from the Gentiles to the poor saints in Jerusalem, he called the offering 'fruit'. 'Therefore, when I have performed this and have sealed to them this fruit, I shall go by way of you to Spain' (Rom. 15:28, NKJV). One of the characteristics of the early Christians was the joyful sharing of their possessions. It was not communism; it was Christian compassion. 'All the believers were together and had everything in common. They sold property and possessions to give to anyone who had need' (Acts 2:44–45). God has not commanded us to follow their exact example, but he has encouraged us to share what we have with others. 'If anyone has material possessions and sees a brother or sister in need but has no pity on them, how can the love of God be in that person?' (1 Jn. 3:17).

Giving to God and, in His name, to others, is not something that we *do*; it is the result of what we *are*. When the branch is receiving life from the Vine, *it cannot help but give*. The branch exists to give! For the branch *giving* and *living* are synonymous. To live is to give; to give is to live. The believer cannot selfishly hold on to whatever material blessings God gives him. If he is abiding in the Vine, he cannot help but give.

Christian character is a fourth kind of fruit, and it is described in Galatians 5:22–23. 'But the fruit of the Spirit is love, joy, peace, forbearance, kindness, goodness, faithfulness, gentleness and self-control …' Who does not want to have these qualities in his life? How different life becomes when you produce the fruit of the spirit. The world has substitutes for these Christian graces, but it cannot duplicate them. Certainly unsaved people enjoy love, but not that deep *agape* love that comes from the heart of God. 'We love because he first loved us' (1 Jn. 4:19). The world manufactures entertainment and even happiness, but it cannot manufacture that deep joy that comes from Christ. You can purchase things to help you *sleep* but you cannot purchase *peace*. All of these marvellous qualities are spiritual fruit that only the Holy Spirit can produce when we, as branches, are drawing upon the life of the Vine.

Each of us wants to improve himself. There are weaknesses in our lives that we want to remove, and there are strengths that we want to develop. How do we do it? *By being branches in the Vine.* As the life of Christ comes in, we find old things passing away and new things taking their place. Just as the face of nature takes on new beauty and power when the spring life comes in, so the Christian experiences new beauty when Christ's life comes in. Christian character – the fruit of the spirit – cannot be manufactured in our own strength. Only the life of Christ within can produce this fruit.

'Bearing fruit in every good work,' (Col. 1:10); this is another kind of spiritual fruit that we bear as His branches. We are not saved by our good works; we are saved 'by grace … through faith' (Ephesians 2:8). But the result of salvation is always service. 'In the same way, let your light shine before others, that they may see your good deeds and glorify your Father in heaven' (Mt. 5:16).

The unsaved person cannot perform any good works. He is dead as far as things spiritual are concerned, and he can only do 'dead works' (Heb. 9:14, NKJV). But when the life of Christ moves in, the result is service for God, 'being fruitful in every good work'. And the beautiful thing about these good works is that *they are tailor-made for each individual believer.* 'For we are God's handiwork, created in Christ Jesus to do good works, which God prepared in advance for us to do' (Eph. 2:10). Each Christian has his own ministry to fulfil, and no Christian is competing with any other Christian in the will of God.

Some of the branches produce their 'good works' fruit in their own homes. Others serve Christ in stores and offices, or even in the cabs of trucks or the cabins of jet planes. The teacher, the builder, the doctor, the city official, the gardener, and the printer – all of these and many more serve Jesus Christ (if they are Christians) by accomplishing the good works he has planned for them. In the Christian life, there is no such division as 'secular' and 'sacred'. 'So whether you eat or drink or whatever you do, do it all for the glory of God' (1 Cor. 10:31). A Christian pilot can serve and glorify the Lord just as much as the missionaries he is flying to the field.

This tremendous truth elevates your vocation, whatever it is, and makes it a ministry for the Lord. Of course, there are some vocations that a believer would not want to enter because in them he could not glorify God. But God can use you in any honourable calling to bring glory to his name. You can be 'fruitful in every good work' and serve Jesus Christ.

Praising and thanking God is another kind of fruit. 'Through Jesus, therefore, let us continually offer to God a sacrifice of praise – the fruit of lips that openly profess his name' (Heb. 13:15). The Old Testament worshipper brought the fruit of his field for a sacrifice to God. The New Testament worshipper brings the fruit of his lips. *By our words, we praise and glorify God.*

Some Christians find it difficult and embarrassing to witness and praise the Lord before others, especially unbelievers. In our own strength, we can never do this; but as branches in the Vine, we can receive His life and bear 'the fruit of lips'. Praising God then becomes a natural thing, not a forced thing, and we do it joyfully and not with a feeling of guilt. A manufactured witness is a dead witness. Praise that is forced is empty praise. But when our words are the fruit of our union with Christ, they are alive and exciting. Our witness has power to it. We do not need to be afraid or ashamed when it comes to sharing Christ with others. God will produce the 'fruit of lips' and others will be able to eat it.

These, then, are some of the different kinds of fruit

God wants us to bear in our lives: witnessing and winning souls, holiness of life, character, sharing, good works, and praise and testimony. But our Lord also makes it clear that this fruitbearing is to be a continuous experience: 'fruit … more fruit … much fruit.' He said, 'This is to my Father's glory, that you bear much fruit, showing yourselves to be my disciples' (Jn. 15:8).

How is this increase possible? There are two answers to the question.

First, as you and I as branches continue to abide in Christ, we establish a deeper relationship with Him. The hindrances that affect the fruitbearing are removed, and He is able to do more in us and through us. The longer we abide in Christ, the better fitted we become to bear more fruit.

Second, the fruit that we bear *has seed in it for more fruit!* As others partake of this fruit, they also begin to bear fruit; and this results in 'more fruit … much fruit …' This points up the difference between 'results' and 'fruit'. It is possible to 'get results' in our Christian service, and even have impressive statistics; but none of these 'results' will bear fruit. It is only as we bear fruit that the seed is there for more fruit.

The following story has been told of both D.L. Moody and Sam Jones, the Methodist evangelist. No matter; the lesson is clear. The evangelist met a drunk on the street, and the drunk said, 'Say, I'm one of your converts!' The evangelist replied, 'You must be one of *my* converts – you certainly aren't one of the Lord's converts.' A good illustration of the difference between 'fruit' and 'results'. Where there is true fruit, there is life; and where there is life, there is the seed for more fruit.

The secret of living is fruitbearing. God did not create you, and Christ did not die for you that you might go through life *getting*. God created you and Christ purchased you that you might invest your life *giving*. If you refuse to bear fruit, you will miss the true meaning and glory of the Christian life. If you yield to Christ and permit His life to create His fruit through you, then you will really live.

Are you willing to be a branch? Tell Him that you are.

Are you willing for His life to work in and through you? Then, tell Him.

By an act of faith, yield yourself to Christ for the purpose of bearing fruit, for the purpose of fulfilling that wonderful plan God has for you and you alone.

Secret Two:

The Secret of
Fruitbearing is Abiding

Abide in Me, and I in you. As the branch cannot bear fruit of itself, unless it abides in the vine, neither can you, unless you abide in Me.

If you abide in Me, and My words abide in you, you will ask what you desire, and it shall be done for you

(Jn. 15:4,7, NJKV)

At least twelve times in the New King James

Version in John 15, Jesus uses the word *abide*. Why? Because abiding is the secret of fruitbearing. The branch does not bear fruit by struggling, but by abiding. If you were to walk through a vineyard, you would not detect tension and struggle among the branches. Instead, you would discover a calm, confident *resting* – an *abiding* – as the branches draw their life from the Vine.

In the Christian life, there is a difference between *union* and *communion*. When you trusted Christ to save you, the Holy Spirit united you to Him in a living relationship. You became a branch in the Vine; a living union was formed. But this once-for-all union is the basis for communion – maintaining a moment-by-moment fellowship with the Lord so that His life is shared with you. The branch that tries to go it alone will never bear fruit.

We must be careful to distinguish between His supernatural life and our own natural qualities. There are many people who by nature are quiet and unassuming, but this attitude is not necessarily Christian humility. Others are naturally optimistic and effervescent, but this may not be Christian joy. How can you tell the difference? In two ways. First, when our abiding in Christ produces true spiritual fruit, *it is beyond anything that we can do and we know it.* Second, because this is true, when there is spiritual fruit, *God gets the glory.* People recognize that it is God at work in our lives doing in and through us what we could never do for ourselves. Certainly the Holy Spirit can use personality traits, such as Peter's courage or Paul's self-control; but usually he has to help us *overcome* these traits when we depend on them and not on the Lord. Peter's courage almost made him a murderer when he struck at Malchus with his sword.

How do we abide in Christ? Historically, two schools of thought have developed around the answer to that important question: the 'quietists' and the 'activists'. The first group says, 'You do nothing. You simply yield to Him and let Him have His way. Christ lives in you and He wants to use you the way the hand uses the glove. All the glove has to do is surrender.' But the second group replies, 'Not on your life! We are not dead gloves but living people. God never violates our personality and forces Himself on us. We must yield, but we must obey as well. We must actively read the Bible, pray, worship, and do all that He wants us to do.'

Actually, both answers contain a measure of truth.

Surrender is important, and cooperation is also important. Abiding is not a passive thing, like a glove on a hand, because a glove does not have intellect, emotions, and will the way a person does. The glove can do nothing else but surrender! On the other hand, abiding is not such an active thing that we must manufacture the experience. Everybody has a 'spiritual formula' for you to follow: A + B + C = D. But formulas for the spiritual life are not always as neat and sure-fire as chemical formulas or cake recipes.

Paul gives us the best answer in Philippians 2:12–13 ' ... continue to work out your salvation with fear and trembling, for it is God who works in you to will and to act in order to fulfil his good purpose.' God works in, we work out. As we surrender, God works in; as we obey, God works out. Abiding involves keeping in fellowship with the Vine so that God can work in us.

Certainly abiding involves spending time with the Lord in meditation and prayer. 'If you abide in Me, and My words abide in you ...' (Jn. 15:7, NKJV). 'If you keep my commandments, you will abide in My love ...' (Jn. 15:10, NKJV). You cannot *keep* his commandments if you do not *know* them, and you cannot know them personally apart from His Word. 'Blessed is the one ... whose delight is in the law of the LORD, and who meditates on his law day and night' (Ps. 1:1–2).

Prayer is also a part of abiding. 'If you abide in Me, and My words abide in you, you will ask what you desire, and it shall be done for you' (Jn. 15:7, NKJV). The better we know the Word of God, the better we can pray; for the Word of God reveals the will of God. 'This is the confidence we have in approaching God: that if we ask anything according to his will, he hears us' (1 Jn. 5:14). Of course, prayer is much more than asking. It also involves giving thanks, expressing love and worship, and also confessing sin.

Confession is a third factor in abiding. Sin always breaks our communion with God. 'If we claim to have fellowship with him and yet walk in the darkness, we lie and do not live out the truth' (1 Jn. 1:6). It is important that we keep our hearts and minds clean and that we confess all known sin. David even asked to be cleansed from 'hidden faults' (Ps. 19:12)! There are sins that we commit that even we may not know about.

A fourth factor is a desire to do his will. ' If you keep My commandments, you will abide in My love' (Jn.

15:10, NKJV). 'I delight to do Your will, O my God,

And Your law is within my heart' (Ps. 40:8). God's will for our lives is that we bear fruit and glorify Him. His plan will be worked out in different ways with different people, and we must be willing for God to have His way. '[N]evertheless, not what I will, but what You will' (Mk. 14:36).

It is the Holy Spirit who encourages and enables us to abide. He teaches us the Word; He enables us to pray; He reveals our sins; He gives us the inward desire to obey God. The Spirit of God uses the Word of God and prayer to strengthen our communion with Christ. This experience of abiding is not always accompanied by 'spiritual feelings' or unusual emotional changes. Then how can we know when we are truly abiding in Christ?

We never have to ask 'Am I abiding in Christ?' because there will be several evidences in our lives when we are in communion with the Lord.

The first evidence, and the most obvious, is *fruit:* 'He who abides in Me, and I in him, bears much fruit; for without Me you can do nothing' (Jn. 15:5, NKJV). If we are maintaining a close fellowship with Him, then the result will be fruit in and through our lives.

We will not need to manufacture 'results' in our own strength. The Holy Spirit will produce fruit, and this fruit will remain.

This means that God will use *us* to touch the lives of others and help win them to Christ. It may not be our privilege to actually lead them to the Saviour, but we will be a part of that miracle experience. My own conversion was the fruit of many different branches, a praying pastor, praying friends, faithful Sunday school teachers, a dedicated evangelist, to name but a few – and when I did trust the Lord, I was standing *alone* in the back of a high school auditorium listening to a man preach! For many years, that evangelist did not know that he had produced fruit in my life that night. In fact, he told me later that he had gone home from the meeting disappointed. God had given some fruit but he did not know it. You may have to wait until you see the Lord in glory before you will know what fruit has been produced in your life.

If you are growing in holy living, and experiencing victory over temptation, then you are abiding in Christ. The *absence* of temptation is not a proof of abiding; the *presence* of temptation and testing is the proof. Bearing 'fruit to holiness' (Rom. 6:22, NKJV) is a daily process, not a finished matter. As we grow in Christ, we conquer new areas in our lives; and the beautiful 'fruit of the Spirit' is more and more evident. If you find yourself growing in 'love, joy, peace, forbearance, kindness, goodness, faithfulness, gentleness and self-control', then you know you are abiding in Christ.

You will also find yourself developing new values and wanting to invest what you have for God's glory. Sharing what we have with others is 'fruit' (Rom.15:28, NKJV). Christians are not only forgiven, but they are also forgiving and *for giving.* 'It is more blessed to give than to receive' (Acts 20:35) is their philosophy of life. The Christian who is not abiding in Christ is selfish; he misses the joy of bearing and sharing.

As you abide in Christ, you will find many ways to work for Him. You will not have to be threatened or bribed: working for Christ will be the natural result of walking with Christ and abiding in Him. You will discover and develop your gifts and go to work in His church as He leads you.

You will find yourself praising the Lord as you abide in Him. You will praise Him for His blessings, and you will praise Him for the burdens of life as well. You will praise Him when the way is bright and clear, and you will praise Him when the way is dark and perplexing.

The Christian who does not abide in Christ gives thanks *occasionally* for *some* things; but the abiding Christian gives thanks *always* for *all* things. Through Christ you will 'continually offer to God a sacrifice of praise,' (Heb. 13:15).

If we do not abide, we do not bear fruit; and if we do not bear fruit, the Father, who is the Vinedresser, must deal with us. ' If anyone does not abide in Me, he is cast out as a branch and is withered; and they gather them and throw them into the fire, and they are burned' (Jn. 15:6, NKJV). Some apply this warning to 'professed' Christians, people who are not truly saved and therefore cannot bear fruit. But how would a 'professed' Christian become a branch of the Vine? When Jesus said 'You are the branches' (Jn. 15:5), he was speaking to saved people who had been cleansed through faith in him (Jn. 15:3). Judas, the counterfeit believer, had already gone out (Jn. 13:21–30).

Is Jesus telling us that, if we do not bear fruit, we lose our salvation? I think not, and for several reasons. To begin with, the emphasis in this message about the vine and the branches is on *service*, not *salvation*. Jesus is not telling us how to get saved, or even how to get others saved, but how to live for Him now that we are saved. The emphasis is on communion, not union; it is on fellowship and discipleship, not sonship. He is addressing us as servants who are His friends (Jn. 15:15), and He is instructing us how to serve Him.

It is God the Father who 'takes away' the branch that does not bear fruit (Jn. 15:1–2). It is not God the Son who does it. God the Father has appointed His Son to be the judge. 'Moreover, the Father judges no one, but has entrusted all judgment to the Son,' (Jn. 5:22). If the consigning of a fruitless branch to the fire meant a soul being sent to eternal judgment, then it would be done by the Son, not the Father.

What is the Father's relationship to the branch? He is the Vinedresser. He seeks to make the branch more fruitful, even to the extent of pruning the branch and cutting away excess wood and leaves (Jn. 15:2). If the branch refuses to abide and bear fruit, then the Father can remove it to make way for a fruitful branch. This is known as spiritual discipline, or chastening. If the branch does not respond to the Father's ministry, then the Father may have to take it away. Paul expressed the same thought in a different context – athletics. 'Everyone who competes in the games goes into strict training ... I strike a blow to my body and make it my slave so that after I have preached to others, I myself will not be disqualified for the prize' (1 Cor. 9:25–27). Is Paul suggesting that he was afraid he might go to hell? I think not. He was telling us of his fear of *losing his ministry and losing his reward*.

No matter how little fruit you may be producing, it is evidence that you are abiding in Christ. The Father sees that fruit and rejoices in it. He then does all He can to help you produce 'more fruit … much fruit' (Jn. 15:2, 5, NKJV). The last thing the Father wants to do is take away your opportunity for glorifying him in fruitbearing. But a fruitless branch is a disgrace to the Vinedresser! Certainly the fruitless believer ought to confess his sins and have his fellowship restored; then he can bear fruit for God's glory.

A second evidence that you are abiding in Christ is *the Father's pruning*. '[E]very branch that does bear fruit he prunes so that it will be even more fruitful' (Jn. 15:2). What is this pruning process? It is the Father cutting out of our lives the things that hinder us from being more fruitful. God also wants us to reach our greatest potential. This explains why abiding Christians are often suffering Christians. They experience the Father's pruning, and it hurts.

What does the Father cut away from our lives?

Anything that keeps the life of the Vine from producing more fruit, much fruit. If the life goes to leaf, He cuts away the excess leaves. Of themselves, leaves are not bad; but if they rob us of fruit, they are sinful. The abiding Christian is not constantly dealing with 'bad things'; he is often dealing with 'good things'. God told Abraham to leave his home and family, but Abraham took his father along. The father had to die before God could continue His work in Abraham's life. But Abraham took his nephew Lot with him, and Lot also had to be cut away. Then it was his son Ishmael, whom he fathered through Hagar. And then it was his beloved son Isaac, who was given to him by the Lord. (Though God gave him back). Expect to be pruned if you abide in Christ.

Have you ever wondered why some believers seem to 'sail through life' in constant sunshine, while others experience suffering and loss? To be sure, God has different plans for each of his children; but this much is true: *believers who abide in Christ can expect to suffer*. The Father's knife is ready to cut away anything in their lives that is keeping them from bearing more fruit for His glory. The Father may *hurt* you, but He will never *harm* you. His pruning is for your good and His glory, and that is all that really counts.

When you first start abiding in Christ, you find the sinful things of your life falling away as His life takes control. It is a thrilling thing to live in victory over the gross things of the flesh and the appetites of the world. But as your experience deepens, you start to experience the pruning process; and God starts to cut away things that you think are good. 'Why, Lord?' is the prayer often on your lips. And His answer is clear: 'I want you to bear more fruit. The secret of living is fruitbearing, and the more fruit you bear, *the more you will live.*' The abiding Christian does not choose between the good and the bad; an unsaved person can do that. The abiding Christian chooses between the better and the best. He is not discouraged when the Father prunes his life and cuts away something that he considers dear, because he knows he will receive something far more precious in return.

Expect to be pruned if you are abiding in Christ. This is the only way to bear more fruit and glorify the Father.

There is a third evidence of abiding; it is *a growing sense of weakness.* 'I am the vine, you are the branches' (Jn. 15:5). The Father often has to remind us that we are *branches* and not the Vine itself. He permits us to go through circumstances that bring out our weakness and His strength. He repeatedly teaches us, 'apart from me, you can do nothing' (Jn.15:5).

This is one reason for the testings that we experience in life. Have you ever noticed that God often tests his children in their strongest points? Satan tempts us in our weakest points to bring out the worst in us, but God tests us in our strongest points to bring out the best in us. If we fail in our *strong* points, think of how much greater we would fail in our weak points!

Abraham's strongest point was his faith, and that is exactly where the Lord tested him. God permitted a famine to come to the land, and Abraham went down to Egypt to save himself. He failed the test. Moses' strongest point was his meekness; yet he lost his temper one day and failed to glorify God. Peter's greatest strength was his courage; yet he became a coward when confronted by a little maid who asked him about Jesus. Peter had boasted that he would even die with the Lord Jesus! He found out how weak he was and that, apart from Christ, he could do nothing.

After you have been abiding in Christ for a long

time, you may be tempted to feel stronger than you really are. You may feel capable of handling life in your own wisdom and power. Beware! You are heading for certain failure and shame. Jesus said, 'apart from me, you can do nothing' (Jn. 15:5). *Nothing.* Of yourself, you are a weak branch, good for nothing but the fire. But in Christ you have all the strength you need to bear fruit and glorify God. *Your weakness is your strength.* God will see to it that you are reminded of your weakness, even if He has to bring you very low to do it. 'Therefore I will boast all the more gladly about my weaknesses, so that Christ's power may rest on me' (2 Cor. 12:9).

If you are abiding in Christ, you will know it because *He will answer your prayers.* 'If you abide in Me, and My words abide in you, you will ask what you desire, and it shall be done for you' (Jn. 15:7, NKJV).

Prayer is not only a *cause* but also a *result* of abiding. As we pray, we abide; as we abide, we pray more, and more deeply. Prayer is not a 'religious exercise' that we perform out of obedience, as good as that might be. Prayer is the very breath and heartbeat of our lives. Prayer is part of a beautiful relationship between us and God: He speaks to us in His Word, and we speak to Him from our hearts. Prayer is not simply a servant showing up for orders from his master. Prayer is a friend sharing his heart with his Friend and growing in love and faith. Jesus does not call us slaves; He calls us friends. Because He is our Friend, we want to talk with Him and listen to Him talk with us.

You dare not separate prayer from the Word of God. 'If you abide in Me, and My words abide in you ...' (Jn. 15:7, NKJV). As we read the Word of God, we discover God's will, what He wants to give us. As we further meditate on His Word, our hearts are gradually changed, and we start to desire what He desires. 'Take delight in the LORD, and he will give you the desires of your heart' (Ps. 37:4). Apart from the inner working of the Word in our hearts, we would never desire what He wants us to desire. Our desires would be selfish and sinful, and our prayers would be selfish and sinful. 'When you ask, you do not receive, because you ask with wrong motives, that you may spend what you get on your pleasures' (Jas. 4:3).

Your Father wants to answer prayer. If you are abiding in Christ, and if His Word abides in you, then you will pray in His will and He will answer. 'This is the confidence we have in approaching God: that if we ask anything according to his will, he hears us' (1 Jn. 5:14). It has well been said that prayer is not getting man's will done in heaven, but getting God's will done on earth. It is not overcoming God's reluctance but laying hold of God's willingness.

If you find your prayers becoming selfish, or if you find prayer becoming a deadening experience, a burden instead of a joy, then it may be that you are not abiding in Christ. If you pray but God does not answer, something may have happened to your communion with Him. 'If I had cherished sin in my heart, the Lord would not have listened;' (Ps. 66:18). Prayer is both a thermometer and a thermostat in the Christian life. It helps to regulate our 'spiritual temperature' but it also registers the devotion of our hearts.

What a joy it is to have God answer prayer! What confidence it gives you to know that you can take 'everything to God in prayer' and He will hear and answer! He does not always give us what we ask, but he does give us what we need, *when we need* it. This is one of the evidences of abiding.

A fifth evidence of abiding is *love for Christ and His people*. 'As the Father loved Me, I also have loved you; abide in My love ... This is My commandment, that you love one another as I have loved you' (Jn. 15:9, 12). God is love, and if we are sharing His life, we must experience His love. And if we experience that love, we must *express* that love to others.

There is a danger that our abiding life may become self-centred and isolated. We get so wrapped up in a relationship with God that we neglect or ignore the people around us. But this kind of 'abiding' is false. The closer we grow to the Lord, the more of His love we will want to share with others. *Christian love is simply treating others the way God has treated us.* Jesus commanded us to 'love one another, just as I have loved you' (Jn. 15:12). 'Dear friends, since God so loved us, we also ought to love one another … We love because he first loved us' (1 Jn. 4:11, 19).

You first experience this love when you trust Christ for salvation: 'God's love has been poured out into our hearts through the Holy Spirit, who has been given to us' (Rom. 5:5). As you abide in Christ, the 'fruit of the Spirit' begins to appear, and the first is love. This Christian love is not a sentimental feeling that comes and goes; no, it is a deep experience through the Spirit that does not fluctuate with changing feelings or circumstances. This love enables us to see Christ in others in spite of their faults and mistakes (1 Pet.

4:8: Above all, love each other deeply, because love covers over a multitude of sins'). There may be people we do not like because of their personalities, or with whom we disagree; but we will love them in Christ.

The test of this love is sacrifice. 'Greater love has no one than this: to lay down one's life for one's friends' (Jn. 15:13). The kind of love our Lord is talking about – *agape* love – is love that gives, that sacrifices, that willingly pays the price that others might be helped. It should be no problem for us to lay down our lives for our friends when Christ laid down his life *for his enemies!*

This *agape* love shines out against the dark background of the world's hatred for Christ and the Christian. 'If the world hates you, keep in mind that it hated me first. If you belonged to the world, it would love you as its own. As it is, you do not belong to the world, but I have chosen you out of the world. That is why the world hates you' (Jn. 15:18–19). By 'the world,' of course Jesus means *society apart from God*, that system of values, philosophies, ideas, goals, and experiences that is wholly separated from God and is even anti-God. He is not speaking about the world of nature or the world of people, although the 'world system' can and does use people and things to promote its cause. The more you abide in Christ, the less you love the world system and the more you love Christ and His people. Conversely, the less you abide in Christ, the more the world will love you, and the less comfortable you will feel with the people of God.

Christians are the light of the world and the salt of the earth (Mt. 5:13–16). Our light shows up the world's darkness; our purity shows up the world's sin. The more we abide in Christ, the brighter the light shines and the purer our lives become, *and the more the world hates us.* 'In fact, everyone who wants to live a godly life in Christ Jesus will be persecuted' (2 Tim. 3:12). Were it not for the love of God's people within the fellowship of the church, we would find it difficult to face the hatred of the world. It is sad when Christians fail to love one another, for that failure makes the church just like the world. If we find ourselves lacking in love for the brethren, it may be a sign we are not abiding in Christ as we should.

When the believer is abiding in Christ, he experiences *an inner joy.*' I have told you this so that my joy may be in you and that your joy may be complete' (Jn. 15:11). Christian joy is not the absence of trial or trouble; it is a deep peace and confidence in the midst of trial and trouble. The very hour in which Jesus spoke those words was one of tremendous pressure and challenge for Him. Judas would betray Him; Peter would deny Him; His own followers would forsake Him and flee. He would be arrested, falsely accused, humiliated, beaten, and then crucified. He would even be forsaken by His Father! *Yet Jesus was able to give His joy to His disciples!* It was a joy in the midst of sorrow, a confidence in the midst of man's failure and sin.

The world offers entertainment, and even a bit of happiness; but only Christ can give joy; and this joy comes from our abiding in him. 'You will fill me with joy in your presence' (Ps. 16:11). 'For the kingdom of God is not a matter of eating and drinking, but of righteousness, peace and joy in the Holy Spirit' (Rom. 14:17). This joy comes from Christ, not from ourselves or the circumstances around us. 'Then my soul will rejoice in the LORD and delight in his salvation.' (Ps. 35:9).

One of the first symptoms of backsliding – not abiding in Christ – is a loss of joy. When David sinned and tried to hide it from God, he ceased to sing and praise the Lord. 'When I kept silent, my bones wasted away through my groaning all day long' (Ps. 32:3). When

David finally confessed his sin, he prayed, 'Restore to me the joy of your salvation' (Ps. 51:12). Spiritual joy is the result of abiding in Christ; loss of that joy is an evidence that we are not abiding in Christ. The only way to restore that communion, and the resulting joy, is through confession. 'If we confess our sins, he is faithful and just and will forgive us our sins and purify us from all unrighteousness' (1 Jn. 1:9).

Here, then, are some of the evidences that we are abiding in Christ: We bear fruit for God's glory. We experience the Father's pruning that we might bear more fruit. We have a sense of weakness and know that we are only the branches; Christ is the Vine. We have our prayers answered. We love the brethren and are hated by the world. We experience a deep joy in spite of circumstances.

To be sure, not every abiding believer will have all of these blessings in the same degree at the same time. But they will be present in some measure, and they will be strong enough to be evident. Others may see these blessings in us better than we do!

It is good for us as branches to examine ourselves regularly to see if we are abiding in Christ. We want to bear fruit, and the secret of fruitbearing is abiding.

Secret Three:

The Secret of Abiding is Obeying

If you keep My commandments, you will abide in My love, just as I have kept My Father's commandments and abide in His love … You are My friends if you do whatever I command you.

(Jn. 15:10,14, NKJV)

It is a fundamental law of the universe, ordained of God, that obedience leads to abiding. The person who obeys the laws of health will abide in health. The farmer

43

who obeys the laws of nature will abide and enjoy the fruits of his labour. The scientist who obeys the laws of science will abide and be able to accomplish things. God has written certain laws and principles into this world, and we cannot disobey them without suffering.

I live not far from one of the world's busiest airports, O'Hare in Chicago. Often I see huge planes taking off and landing, and I never cease to marvel at the fact that those gigantic machines can ever get off the ground and stay in the air. The law of gravity dictates that it cannot be done. But by obeying other laws, the aeronautical engineers can make the planes fly. If the pilot stops obeying, he stops abiding!

One reason we are facing ecological problems and crises is because we did not obey God's laws. Had we obeyed, we would still be abiding in a world with plenty of pure air and water and a growing supply of natural resources. But we did not obey, so we cannot abide. *The secret of abiding is obeying.*

Why is this so? Why did God make obedience the secret of abiding?

To begin with, *God obeys His own laws.*

There are times when he performs miracles and brings a higher law into play, but God's usual mode of working is to obey His own laws that He has built into the universe. Because He does obey these laws, we have the changes of seasons, we have harvests, and we can harness the tremendous power that the universe holds. All of science is based on the fact that God obeys His own laws. From the splitting of the atom to the charting of a distant planet, man can depend on God's laws. If God once disobeyed his own laws, the universe would fall apart.

The source of evil in this world is man, not God. It was because of the first man's disobedience to God's law that sin came into the world. It is because men and women continue to disobey God's will that evil grows and destroys in this world. The same divine law that gives the farmer corn when he plants corn also gives the sinner sorrow and death when he sins, for we reap what we sow. 'Do not be deceived: God cannot be mocked. A man reaps what he sows. Whoever sows to please their flesh, from the flesh will reap destruction; whoever sows to please the Spirit, from the Spirit will reap eternal life' (Gal. 6:7–8).

Since God obeys His own laws, and the universe abides in Him because He does, then when we obey His Word, we too will abide in Him. To disobey

God is to fly in the face of the whole universe! This explains why the disobedient person has so much trouble, not only inwardly, but also outwardly. When the child of God obeys the will of God, everything in the world works for him, but when the child of God disobeys the will of God, everything works against him. There are times when *obedience* seems to bring difficulty; but the trial is only temporary, and the result will be blessing. Paul and Silas obeyed God in going to Philippi, and ended up in prison. But the result was great blessing in the salvation of the jailer and his family, and the establishing of a new church.

Everything in the universe obeys God except man, and man has the most to gain by obeying and the most to lose by disobeying! The biggest stars and the tiniest cells all obey God's will. This is what keeps the universe together: 'lightning and hail, snow and clouds, stormy winds that do his bidding' (Ps. 148:8). No part of His natural creation would ever think of questioning God's will, let alone disobeying it. Only man questions and disobeys God's will, because man (by God's grace) has a will of his own. He was created to make decisions, and he can decide to disobey God.

This is the second reason why obedience is the secret of abiding: *obedience involves the will*. We do not abide simply by having thoughts about God's will or even feelings about God's will. We abide when we obey God's will, and this means submitting our will. Of course, we ought to do the will of God from the heart, and we ought to be intelligent about it; but the important thing is *doing it*. No amount of thoughts in the mind and feelings in the heart can compensate for disobedience of the will.

Too many Christians settle for an intellectual experience. They study the Bible, learn facts and definitions, and try to explain doctrines; but they never obey what God tells them. Other believers have only an emotional experience: they try to generate and cultivate 'spiritual feelings' that help them 'enjoy the Lord'. While sincere emotion is certainly a part of the Christian life, it is not the only part.

We must realize that *the will* is the centre of the Christian life. We obey God, not because we feel like it, but because it is the right thing to do. And we should graduate from obeying *because we have to* into obeying *because we want to*. Jonah finally obeyed God; but deep within, he still wanted his own way. 'Doing the will of God from the heart' (Eph. 6:6) is the best description of the kind of obedience God is seeking.

Our Lord uses Himself as the example of obedience. 'If you keep My commandments, you will abide in My love, just as I have kept My Father's commandments and abide in His love' (Jn. 15:10, NKJV). '"My food," said Jesus, "is to do the will of him who sent me and to finish his work"' (Jn. 4:34). 'I seek not to please myself but him who sent me' (Jn. 5:30). 'For I have come down from heaven not to do my will but to do the will of him who sent me' (Jn. 6:38). 'I desire to do your will, my God; your law is within my heart (Ps. 40:8).

Because the Son loved the Father, He obeyed His will, no matter what the cost. Jesus did not permit people to turn Him from the will of God. When Peter suggested that Jesus not go to the cross, Jesus replied, 'Get behind me, Satan! You are a stumbling block to me; you do not have in mind the concerns of God, but merely human concerns' (Mt. 16:23). Our Lord's obedience to the will of God cost Him His life. 'He humbled himself by becoming obedient to death – even death on a cross!' (Phil. 2:8). This is what He meant by 'taking up a cross'. He meant obedience in spite of suffering, shame, and sacrifice.

You and I will do everything possible to avoid obedience. And yet obedience is the very key to God's blessing. King Saul tried to substitute sacrifice for obedience, but God would not accept the substitute (1 Sam. 15:22). Jesus told a story about two sons who were given orders by their father, and one of the boys substituted words for obedience (Mt. 21:28–32). His words were not accepted. In His parable of the talents (Mt. 25:14–30), Jesus told about a one-talent man who tried to substitute excuses for disobedience; and he was judged. *There is no substitute for obedience.*

As God's children, we should want to obey Him so that we might abide in Him. The blessings we receive come from the abiding, just as the abiding comes from the obeying. These blessings are not a reward for obeying; they are a result of abiding. We must never bargain with God. We must never say, 'Lord I will obey what you command if You will do for me what I want done.' Our obedience must be complete and unconditional. 'What shall I do, Lord?' (Acts 22:10).

The tragic results of disobedience are recorded in the Bible, beginning with man's first rebellion in Genesis 3. Adam and Eve did not abide because they did not obey. In spite of occasional failures, Abraham obeyed God and maintained his fellowship with Him. Abraham became 'God's friend' (Jas. 2:23), while Lot became a friend of the world. The nation of Israel disobeyed God and did not abide in their land. First they were carried to Babylon; then they were scattered throughout the world. 'See, I am setting before you today a blessing and a curse – the blessing if you obey the commands of the LORD your God that I am giving you today; the curse if you disobey the commands of the LORD your God' (Deut. 11:26–28).

Obedience releases power. When the scientist obeys the laws of science, built into nature by God, then he can release power. The farmer who obeys the laws of growth will release power and produce fruit. But when we disobey these laws, the power that is released will destroy us and not help us. Disobey the laws that govern electricity and you may kill yourself and others. Obey them, and you will abide.

But obeying is one of the most difficult things in the world! There is something perverse and selfish in our very nature that tells us, 'Do it your own way! Don't bow down to anybody else!' We inherited this stubbornness from our first parents, and they got it by listening to Satan's, 'Did God really say … ?' (Gen. 3:1). Paul described our sad plight: 'For I know that good itself does not dwell in me, that is, in my sinful nature. For I have the desire to do what is good, but I cannot carry it out. For I do not do the good I want to do, but the evil I do not want to do – this I keep on doing.' (Rom. 7:18–19).

How can you and I obey God?

That is our next secret.

Secret Four:

The Secret of Obeying is Loving

As the Father loved Me, I also have loved you; abide in My love. If you keep My commandments, you will abide in My love, just as I have kept My Father's commandments and abide in His love.

(Jn. **15:9–10**, NKJV)

If anyone loves Me, he will keep My word ...

He who does not love Me does not keep My words ...

(Jn.**14:23, 24**, NKJV)

If you love Me, keep My commandments.

(Jn.14:15, NKJV)

There are three levels of obedience.

We can obey God because *we have to;* this is the level of fear. There is, of course, a proper fear of God that is holy and good. It is not the fear that a slave shows to a master, but the respect that a son shows to a father.

'Moreover, we have all had human fathers who disciplined us and we respected them for it. How much more should we submit to the Father of spirits and live!' (Heb. 12:9). If we wilfully disobey God, He will chasten us. For this reason, we fear Him.

But fear is not the best motive for obedience. 'I no longer call you servants,' said Jesus to His disciples (Jn. 15:15), indicating that their relationship was much deeper. Fear can rob us of the real joys that God wants us to experience because we obey Him. Because we are His children, we want to get closer to Him; and fear builds walls instead of bridges.

The next level of obedience is selfishness: we obey because *we need to*, because we get something out of it! Peter illustrates this level when he asked

Jesus, 'We have left everything to follow you! What then will there be for us?' (Mt. 19:27). Children obey their parents because children are afraid of being told off. Teenagers obey because they have learned that obedience can purchase favours! The young man who mows the lawn and cleans his room is going to have a better chance to get the keys to the car. And the girl who has helped mother in the kitchen is going to have a better chance to go shopping for new clothes. Selfish? Yes – but it works!

Many Christians live on this 'bargain basement' level. Their obedience is measured by what God gives them; and if they do not get what they want, they often turn against God. They do not have the kind of obedience shown by the three Hebrews when Nebuchadnezzar threatened to throw them into the blazing furnace. ' If we are thrown into the blazing furnace, the God we serve is able to deliver us from it, and he will deliver us from Your Majesty's hand. But even if he does not, we want you to know, Your Majesty, that we will not serve your gods or worship the image of gold you have set up' (Dan. 3:17–18).

The highest motive for obedience is *love*. 'If you love me, keep my commands' (Jn. 14:15).

Why is love the highest motive for obedience?

For one thing, love centres on the giver, not the gift. Love establishes a personal relationship with God no matter what He gives or what He withholds. Satan was sure that Job would curse God when Job lost his possessions and his health. If Job had been like some believers today, that is exactly what he would have done. Instead, he testified, 'Though he slay me, yet will I hope in him … ' (Job 13:15). Where there is love, there can be no bargaining. Jacob, the greater schemer and bargainer, forgot about the contract when he fell in love with Rachel! He willingly worked fourteen years to make her his own; 'they seemed like only a few days to him because of his love for her' (Gen. 29:20).

Another reason is this: love does not measure sacrifice. 'Greater love has no one than this: to lay down one's life for one's friends' (Jn. 15:13). Our Lord proved His love for us by going to the cross for us. He did not measure His sacrifice and give the least possible amount. He gave His all. If we love God, we do not measure the cost of obeying His Word. We simply obey. Like the father that rushes into the burning house to save his child, or the mother that plunges into the raging waters, we do not count the cost, but instead obey the loving impulses of the heart. Love that calculates is not true love.

Love is the highest motive for obedience because 'God is love' (1 Jn. 4:8). He gives His commandments because He loves us; and because we love Him, we obey His commandments. We do not question them or seek to change them. We do not fear His will. 'There is no fear in love. But perfect love drives out fear ...' (1 Jn. 4:18). As we obey, we experience the love of God in our hearts in a deep and satisfying way. 'God is love, and he who abides in love abides in God, and God in him' (1 Jn. 4:16, NKJV). 'Whoever has my commands and keeps them is the one who loves me. The one who loves me will be loved by my Father, and I too will love them and show myself to them' (Jn. 14:21).

Love is the fulfilment of the law. If two people love each other, they do not need rules and regulations to govern their relationship. When a husband and wife love each other, they always try to do the things that please each other and help each other. There are laws that require mothers and fathers to care for their children, but no loving parent ever thinks of those laws! Parents care for their children because they love them.

God wants obedience *from the heart*. It is this truth that underlies the Book of Deuteronomy. The word means 'second law,' since in Deuteronomy Moses repeats the law for the new generation about to enter Canaan. But Deuteronomy is different from Exodus, because Deuteronomy emphasizes *the heart*. The word *love* is introduced in this book, because love is the motive for obeying the law. In Exodus, the emphasis is on judgment and fear; but in Deuteronomy the emphasis is on blessing and love. Of course, there are in this book warnings against sin; but the main theme is love.

Why did God choose Israel?

'Because he loved your ancestors and chose their descendants after them' (Deut. 4:37).

What is Israel's confession of faith?

'Hear, O Israel: The LORD our God, the LORD is one. Love the LORD your God with all your heart and with all your soul and with all your strength' (Deut. 6:4–5).

Is Israel better than any other nation?

'The LORD did not set his affection on you and choose you because you were more numerous than other peoples, for you were the fewest of all peoples. But it was because the LORD loved you and kept the oath he swore to your ancestors … ' (Deut. 7:7–8).

What does God require of his people?

'And now, Israel, what does the LORD your God ask of you but to fear the LORD your God, to walk in obedience to him, to love him, to serve the LORD your God with all your heart and with all your soul' (Deut. 10:12). 'Love the LORD your God and keep his requirements, his decrees, his laws and his commands always' (Deut. 11:1).

But is it not enough that Israel is circumcised? 'The LORD your God will circumcise your hearts and the hearts of your descendants, so that you may love him with all your heart and with all your soul, and live' (Deut. 30:6).

Moses makes it clear to Israel – and to us – that the secret of obeying is loving. It is no wonder that Deuteronomy was our Lord's favourite book when He was here on earth. He quoted from it more than from any other. In the entire New Testament, Deuteronomy is quoted or referred to over eighty times. It is the book of loving obedience and obedient love.

You and I cannot command others to love us, yet God commands us to love Him! He has the right to command us because He always must will for us that which is the highest and the best. Furthermore, 'God's commandments are God's enablements.' By his very commanding, He assures us that this love is possible. Of ourselves, we cannot love Him. 'Apart from me you can do nothing' (Jn. 15:5). But 'I can do all this through him who gives me strength' (Phil. 4:13).

It is possible for us to love Him, and to love Him more and more. And the more we love Him, the more we will obey Him. The more we obey Him, the more we will abide in Him. And the more we abide in Him, the more we will bear fruit. And the more we bear fruit, *the more we will live!*

There is a secret to loving.

Secret Five:

The Secret of Loving is Knowing

I no longer call you servants, because a servant does not know his master's business. Instead, I have called you friends, for everything that I learned from my Father I have made known to you.

(Jn. 15:15)

My hobby is reading biographies. I have hundreds of them in my library, and some of them I have read many times. There are a few famous preachers, for example, that interest me greatly, and I have every biography of them that I can find. The better I get to know them, the more I appreciate them.

However, I have biographies of a few great men (not preachers) whose lives utterly disgust me. The better I get to know them, the more I wish I had never heard of them!

Phillips Brooks used to say that 'familiarity breeds contempt only with contemptible things or contemptible people.' He is right. I cannot conceive of familiarity breeding contempt in the lives of a loving husband and wife who have shared a home for fifty years. At most golden wedding anniversary celebrations, the couple usually says, 'We know each other better today then ever before, and we love each other more!'

The better you know Jesus Christ, the more you will love Him. Your first knowledge of Jesus Christ was in connection with your salvation. 'Now this is eternal life: that they know you, the only true God, and Jesus Christ, whom you have sent' (Jn. 17:3). But salvation is only the beginning. It is our privilege and joy to 'grow in the grace and knowledge of our Lord and Saviour Jesus Christ' (2 Pet. 3:18). The Apostle Paul had been a Christian at least twenty-five years when he wrote to the church at Philippi, 'I want to know Christ' (Phil. 3:10). And Paul had visited the third heaven!

Why is it important for us to get to know Christ better? For one thing, salvation is a living relationship, and we cannot grow as Christians apart from the personal fellowship with the Saviour. It is easy for us to substitute other things – even good things – for this personal fellowship with Christ. We must beware of a second-hand relationship. Every book we read, every meeting we attend, every spiritual contact we make must in some way add to our personal knowledge of Jesus Christ. The better we get to know Him, the more we grow in the Christian life and experience maturity.

But something else is true: the better we know Him, the more we become like Him. Just as two friends gradually become alike, or a husband and wife gradually grow together, so the believer and the Saviour grow together as they fellowship with each other. Moses met God on the mountaintop and came down with the glory on his face, a glory that faded away. We have Christ *living within;* and as we commune with Him, His glory radiates through us. God's purpose for our lives is that we might be 'conformed to the image of his Son' (Rom. 8:29). Of course, when Jesus Christ returns, we shall be like Him (1 John 3:1–2); but we can start becoming like Him today. The better you get to know Him, the more you become like Him.

There is a third result of knowing Christ better: you get to know yourself better, and you become your best self. Learning more about Jesus Christ does not make you less of a person; rather, it brings out of you all that God has put in you for His glory. The amazing thing about the Christian life is that we Christians all seek to be more like Christ, yet we are not imitating one another! Becoming like Christ is a process that helps us become ourselves and fulfil the purposes God has for us. Each of the twelve apostles was different, yet each of them accomplished God's will in his own assigned way.

So, getting to know Christ better leads to spiritual growth, which makes us more like Christ and helps us become all that He wants us to become. But there is another wonderful result of growing in your knowledge of Christ: *the better you know Him, the more you love Him*. The secret of obeying is loving, and the secret of loving is knowing.

Jesus Christ wants us to know Him better. This is why he calls us 'friends' and not 'slaves'. No master stoops to explain his plans to a slave; but a friend shares his heart and mind with those who are dear to him. The word that Jesus uses for 'friends' is used in Greek literature for 'an intimate at court'. We are friends of the King! He wants to share Himself and His plans with us.

As you read the Gospel records in the New Testament, you see how patiently and lovingly our Lord revealed Himself and His plans to His disciples. At times the disciples were disgustingly ignorant and almost unteachable. Often He had to bring them to the end of themselves before they were willing to listen and learn. Jesus knew just how much they could take and when they were ready for a new lesson. 'I have much more to say to you, more than you can now bear' (Jn. 16:12).

Because He is our Friend, we can go to Him, talk with Him, and listen to Him. Christ wants to share with us all that He has heard from the Father. This He does through His Word, by His Spirit. 'But when he, the Spirit of truth, comes, he will guide you into all the truth … ' (Jn. 16:13). As you read the Word, meditate on it, pray over it, and ask the Spirit to guide you, then you get to know Christ better.

No matter where you turn in the Word, you meet

Jesus Christ. 'And beginning with Moses and all the Prophets, he explained to them what was said in all the Scriptures concerning himself' (Lk. 24:27). He is seen in type and prophecy in the Old Testament. He is seen ministering on earth in the Gospels, and ministering through His church in the book of Acts. The epistles interpret for us the spiritual truths contained in the Person and work of Christ. The book of Revelation depicts Him as the slain Lamb, the Judge, and the King of Kings. The theme of the whole Bible is Jesus Christ the Son of God.

One of the benefits of Christian fellowship is the opportunity for others to help us learn more about Christ. Believers who have walked with Him longer than we have can tell us much about the Saviour and His gracious working in their lives. We, in turn, can encourage others with our own witness. Where even two or three believers are gathered in His name, He is there to reveal Himself.

As we grow spiritually, we also see Him in nature and history as well as in the Word. To be sure, the Bible is the primary source of spiritual knowledge about God; but it is still true that 'The heavens declare the glory of God' (Ps. 19:1). When He was here on earth, Jesus saw the hand of God in the lilies and the birds. He took the common things of life, like water, bread, seed, and even children, and from them taught profound lessons about God. When you have the Word of God in your heart, you can look at creation and see the hand of God at work.

So, the better you know Christ, the more you will love Him. When you begin to understand the glory of His person and the wonder of His work, you will worship and adore Him. He will become the pre-eminent one in your life. Your love for Him will not obliterate your love for others: it will sanctify your love and enrich it. We must not love our family, for example, more than we love Christ; but the more we love Christ, the more love we will show to our family *to the glory of God*. As your love for Christ grows, your love for others will be purified; the selfishness will be taken away.

But the more you love Christ, the more you will obey Him. And the more you obey Him, the more you will abide in Him. As you abide in Him, you will bear fruit; and the more you bear fruit, *the more you will live!*

It all begins with your knowing Christ in a deeper way, because the secret of loving is knowing.

> *Therefore, I urge you, brothers and sisters, in view of God's mercy, to offer your bodies as a*

living sacrifice, holy and pleasing to God – this is your true and proper worship. Do not conform to the pattern of this world, but be transformed by the renewing of your mind. Then you will be able to test and approve what God's will is –his good, pleasing and perfect will.

(Rom. 12:1–2)

Down through the centuries, men and women of God have made an important discovery. They have discovered that, if they are going to be fruitful for the Lord, they must spend time with Him each day. Some Christians call this their 'quiet time'; others know it as 'personal devotions'. No matter what name you give it, the experience is an important one.

When our Lord was ministering on earth, He started each day with this kind of fellowship with His Father. 'Very early in the morning, while it was still dark, Jesus got up, left the house and went off to a solitary place, where he prayed' (Mk. 1:35). The Messianic passage in Isaiah 50 gives us some insight into what Jesus did. 'He wakens me morning by morning, wakens my ear to listen like one being instructed' (Is. 50:4). Jesus spent the early hours of the day talking to His Father and listening to His Father.

Successful Christians of all ages have learned that secret. If you start your day with the Lord, you may abide in Him all day and experience the joy of bearing fruit. It demands discipline, to be sure; but it is the kind of discipline that becomes a spiritual dynamic.

If you want to know Christ better, abide in Him, and enjoy a fruitful life, then determine to have a disciplined and satisfying devotional life.

What are the elements involved in such a life? They are given to us in Romans 12:1–2, the verses quoted at the beginning of this chapter.

1. Give God your body.

When you first awaken in the morning, simply give your body to God – *and then get up!* Like the soldier hearing reveille, get up! Selfish indulgence of the body often leads to sinful indifference later in the day. Follow the example of Paul who said, 'Everyone who competes in the games goes into strict training … I strike a blow to my body and make it my slave …' (1 Cor. 9:25, 27). God wants to use your body to bear fruit for His glory. He wants His life to work in and through your body. By faith, give Him your body as your first step in worship each day.

2. Give God your mind.

He wants to transform you by renewing your mind. How does he do this? *Through His Word*. Reach for your Bible, read it, and let the Spirit of God teach you. Where should you read in your Bible? I suggest that you adopt a plan for reading through the Bible. I like to start in Genesis 1, Psalm 1, and Matthew 1, and keep reading. I do not always read three chapters a day. Sometimes God stops me at one verse! But you will want to have a systematic plan for reading through the Bible. Do not try to do it in any given time; let the Lord set the pace for you.

Meditation is to the heart and mind what digestion is to the body. Some people read the Bible the way they read a cookbook, and you can starve that way! Take time to let the Spirit reveal Christ to you in the Word. The Holy Spirit is your teacher. If you yield to Him and ask for His help, He will open the Word to you. When you learn a spiritual truth, receive it into your inner self. Make it a part of your 'spiritual muscles'. As the Lord gradually changes and transforms your mind, you will know Christ better and love Him more.

3. Give God your will.

' ...Then you will be able to test and approve what

God's will is ...' (Rom. 12:2). How do you give God your will? *Through prayer.* As you pray, you yield your will to God. You tell Him that He can do in and through you whatever He knows is best. Prayer involves many things: confessing sin, asking for God's help, interceding for others. But basically prayer is saying, 'Yet not as I will, but as you will' (Mt. 26:39).

Many people have found it helpful to have a prayer list. It helps them remember their requests. I like to keep several prayer lists, in fact, one for each day of the week. This keeps me from praying for the same things in a ritual way each day. It also enables me to pray about more needs and more people. There are some items that I remember each day, and the Lord always brings new requests to my attention as I pray. Whatever approach you use, be systematic in your praying; and it will not hurt to keep a record of the way God has answered.

4. Give God your heart.

Worship him. Love him. Be silent before Him in your love. Do not try to manufacture a 'spiritual feeling'. We worship God 'in spirit and truth' (Jn. 4:24). A friend and I were taking a long trip together, and for many miles we said nothing to each other. Then my friend said, 'You know, it's good to have the kind of relationship that isn't shattered by silence!' Often, as my wife and I drive together, we say nothing; and then when we do speak, we find we are thinking about the same things. You can have a similar relationship with the Lord as you worship Him and love Him from our heart.

These are the elements involved in a satisfying devotional life: each morning give God your body, mind, will, and heart.

You can see how these four elements work together with the five secrets I have been sharing with you. The secret of living is fruitbearing, and the secret of fruitbearing is abiding.

What is the secret of abiding?
It is *obeying*; give God *your will*.

What is the secret of obeying?
It is *loving*; give God *your heart*.

What is the secret of loving?
It is *knowing*; give God *your mind*.

In other words, when you surrender heart, mind, and will to God each day, you are able to abide in Him and draw upon His spiritual power. When you yield Him your body, He can work through you to produce the spiritual fruit that He wants you to bear. Instead of being 'conformed to this world', you are *transformed* by his power – and you glorify His name.

I cannot emphasize too much the importance of this daily quiet time with the Lord. But I must add that meeting God in the morning also means that you fellowship with Him all day long. At different times during the day, you will find the Holy Spirit speaking to you. *Listen!* There will be occasions when your heart will reach out for God. *Pause and love Him!* It is as you abide in Him all day long that He is able to work in and through you. This is how you bear fruit.

> *Catch for us the foxes, the little foxes that ruin the vineyards.*

> **(Song 2:15)**

As you begin to abide in Christ and become a fruitful branch, you must watch out for enemies. If you do not, you will begin to lose your fruitfulness.

As the Vinedresser, your Father wants to keep the branches clean. Dirty branches and leaves can hinder fruitfulness. The Father keeps you clean through his Word. 'You are already clean because of the word I have spoken to you' (Jn. 15:3). In the Bible, water for drinking is a picture of the Holy Spirit (Jn. 7:37–39); but water for washing is a picture of God's Word. As you read His Word, it reveals your heart; it cleanses your mind. If God shows you some uncleanness, you can confess it and receive His promised forgiveness (1 Jn. 1:9).

Along with dirt, there are insects and diseases that can bring blight and even death. These the Father must remove. Sometimes He must cut away a diseased part in order to spare the healthy parts. You and I may not enjoy this surgery, but it is good for us. It has been said that the Father is never so near to the branch as when He is pruning it. He may hurt us, but He will never harm us.

The 'little foxes' can also ruin the vineyard. Foxes usually feed on small animals, but they also eat fruit. They are not too careful in the way they steal the fruit, and thus they damage the branches. In the Christian life, it is usually the little things that rob us of blessing. It is not necessary for a herd of cattle to trample the vineyard, or a fire to burn it. The 'little foxes' can destroy it, if only given enough time.

Take, for example, some of the 'little sins' that we fail to deal with: impatience, criticism, short temper, fussiness, and questionable humour. These may be 'faults' or 'sins in good standing' in the eyes of men, but what are they in the eyes of God? It seemed a little thing for King David to leave the battlefield and return to the palace for a rest; but that little bit of indulgence led him into adultery and murder. It was just a 'little nap' that Peter took in the garden, but his lack of watching and praying led to his shameful denials of Christ.

The little foxes spoil the vines, so watch for them *and kill them!* Name the sins, confess them, and ask for God's forgiveness. Never feed a 'little fox.' He will grow up and devour you!

In takes diligence and dedication to bear fruit for God. Once we become lazy and careless, we cease to bear fruit. Solomon paints a meaningful picture of this truth in Proverbs 24:30–34.

> *I went past the field of a sluggard,*
>
>> *past the vineyard of someone who has no sense;*
>
> *thorns had come up everywhere,*
>
>> *the ground was covered with weeds,*
>>
>> *and the stone wall was in ruins.*
>
> *I applied my heart to what I observed*

and learned a lesson from what I saw:
A little sleep, a little slumber,
a little folding of the hands to rest –
and poverty will come on you like a thief
and scarcity like an armed man.

'A little sleep – a little slumber'.

'The little foxes that are ruining the vineyards'.

Deal with sin while it is little! Otherwise, it will grow and do great damage, and rob you of your fruitfulness.

Too much self-analysis and introspection is not good. But it is good for us to search our hearts and confess our sins to God. It is good to uncover the 'little foxes' before they destroy us. '[L]et us purify ourselves from everything that contaminates body and spirit, perfecting holiness out of reverence for God' (2 Cor. 7:1).

And another angel came out from the altar, who
had power over fire, and he cried with a loud cry
to him who had the sharp sickle, saying, 'Thrust
in your sharp sickle and gather the clusters of the
vine of the earth, for her grapes are fully ripe.'
So the angel thrust his sickle into the earth and

gathered the vine of the earth, and threw it into
the great winepress of the wrath of God.

(Rev. 14:18–19, NKJV)

'The vine of the earth!'

This is God's description of society without Christ. Those who have trusted Christ are branches in the Vine of heaven. Those who have rejected Him are branches in the vine of earth.

And they are destined for judgment.

This present world system looks fruitful and successful. Unbelievers tell us that 'things are getting better and better'. But God sees the 'vine of the earth' ripening for His wrath. The clusters will be cut off and the fruit cast into the winepress of the wrath of God.

If you have trusted Christ as your Saviour, then you do not belong to this 'vine of the earth'. You are a branch in the true Vine from heaven.

If you have never trusted Christ, then you are a part of the 'vine of the earth', and you are destined for judgment.

BUT – you can escape that judgment!

Listen to God's good news for you.

'For God so loved the world that he gave his one

and only Son, that whoever believes in him shall not perish but have eternal life' (Jn. 3:16).

Whoever – that includes you.

Believes – that also includes you.

Trust Christ! Yield yourself to Him!

Today, abandon the 'vine of the earth' and, by faith, become a branch in the true Vine. Start living! Start bearing fruit for God's Glory!

'Everyone who calls on the name of the Lord will be saved'

(Rom. 10:13).